India

LAND OF LIVING TRADITIONS

Photographs by Michael Freeman

Essays by Alistair Shearer

PERIPLUS

Published by Periplus Editions with editorial offices at 364 Innovation Drive, North
Clarendon, Vermont 05759 U.S.A and 61 Tai Seng Avenue, #02-12, Singapore 534167

Library of Congress Control Number: 2008927101

ISBN 978-0-7946-0602-2

Distributed by
North America, Latin America and Europe
Tuttle Publishing
364 Innovation Drive, North Clarendon, VT 05759-9436, USA
Tel: 1 (802) 773-8930; Fax: 1 (802) 773-6993
info@tuttlepublishing.com
www.tuttlepublishing.com

Japan
Tuttle Publishing
Yaekari Building, 3rd Floor; 5-4-12 Osaki
Shinagawa-ku; Tokyo 141 0032
Tel: (81) 03 5437-0171; Fax: (81) 03 5437-0755
tuttle-sales@gol.com

Asia Pacific
Berkeley Books Pte. Ltd.
61 Tai Seng Avenue #02-12, Singapore 534167
Tel: (65) 6280-1330; Fax: (65) 6280-6290
inquiries@periplus.com.sg
www.periplus.com.sg

Printed in Malaysia

12 11 10 09 08   10 9 8 7 6 5 4 3 2 1

Front endpaper: A modern mural on the walls of the Udaivlas resort in Udaipur
depicts in the traditional Rajasthani style a procession led by oxen.
Back endpaper: A detail of pietra dura at the Taj Mahal, Agra.
Right: A painter in Cochin continues the Indian tradition of giant hand-painted
posters, this one advertising perfume.
Opposite: In the foothills of the Himalayas, yoga classes take place in the open pavil-
ion of a palace in Rishikesh.

Contents

"The sole country under the sun that is endowed with imperishable interest...the one land all men desire to see, and having seen once, by even a glimpse, would not give that glimpse for the shows of all the rest of the globe combined."

—Mark Twain, ninteenth-century American writer and traveller.

Introduction

India is not just another country—it is an extraordinary adventure. Nowhere else has the same power to ravage the senses, strain the credibility, expand the mind and open the heart as this teeming kaleidoscope of seeming contradictions, a land full of contrasts as legion as they are legendary. It is the living museum of the human mind; to journey here is to time travel among sights, beliefs and practices that have long since disappeared elsewhere. Nothing is hidden in India. She is the land of dreams and tales, where travelling storytellers still mesmerize their village audiences, yet she is simultaneously the world's biggest inventor of sophisticated computer software. A fabulous, ancient and stately civilisation, where respected feudal rulers still live in palaces and millions hold the cow sacred, India somehow manages to be the world's largest democracy, which, while only 52 per cent literate, contains the world's second largest pool of trained scientists and engineers.

Everywhere one looks in India, time-hallowed tradition meets the twenty-first century head-on in a dizzying cocktail of intense impressions. Peacocks sit imperiously atop satellite dishes; elephants and cows cause good-natured traffic jams; processions of naked ascetics amble

past crowded cybercafes. All humanity seems to be on the move on India's roads, where the latest Mercedes jostles with wooden bullock-carts designed five thousand years ago and painted trucks, vertiginously laden, lurch past brilliant swathes of cotton, silk and chillies spread out to dry in the scorching sun beneath impossible tangles of telephone wires. The city streets, sizzling with entrepreneurial energy, are packed with people, yet beyond the cities lie the somnolent villages where seven out of every ten Indians live and time hangs suspended; beyond them again stretch tranquil forests and silent deserts where wild animals still reign.

India's uniqueness has attracted adventurers—merchants, poets, artists—for millennia; today's tourists are merely the latest wave of visitors to stand and marvel. This is a civilisation that has suffered and absorbed innumerable foreign conquests, creating a a richly variegated tapestry of peoples and traditions, yet it is today facing perhaps the greatest threat to its survival. For traditionally India—and this is part of her fascination—has stood for values that are very different to those of the modern, secular West. She has believed that humanity is inextricably part of nature, not merely its exploiter; that human communities—family, tribe, caste—have enduring value, not just their individual members; that the worlds of the imagination, the hidden realms of gods, myths and magic, are just as real as the daylight world of history and science. Above all she has taught that we should lead a tolerant and balanced life in rhythms well-established, the goal of which is not merely to accumulate money, power and things, but to find God. In the brave new world of globalisation and the Internet, what is unique in India may not survive for long, yet it may be that she has things to teach us.

Scenes from the annual parade of painted elephants, just before the festival of Holi in the city of Jaipur.

Left: Man Mandir Palace, Gwalior. Built between 1486 and 1517 by Raja Mansingh, the palace dominates Gwalior Fort, which stands on a steep mass of sandstone overlooking the city.
Above: Cut into the sandstone cliffs below Gwalior Fort are a series of Jain statues. These are in the best-preserved southeast group.

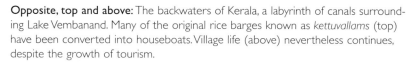

Opposite, top and above: The backwaters of Kerala, a labyrinth of canals surrounding Lake Vembanand. Many of the original rice barges known as *kettuvallams* (top) have been converted into houseboats. Village life (above) nevertheless continues, despite the growth of tourism.

Top: A misty sunrise over harvested rice fields in the southern state of Tamil Nadu.
Above: Farmers winnowing rice during the harvest following the monsoon rains in a village near Mamallapuram, south of Chennai.

Fatehpur Sikri, 'the City of Victory,' was built by the Mughal emperor Akbar in 15 years, starting in about 1569. Sheikh Salim Chishti's white marble mausoleum is the jewel of the courtyard of the Friday Mosque.

The tomb of Itmad-ud-Daulah was built on the banks of the Yamuna River in Agra between 1622 and 1625. It includes many design features that were later used in the construction of the nearby Taj Mahal.

The Taj Hotel in Mumbai is one of the city's enduring landmarks. Built in 1903, it was the first modern hotel in the city, then known as Bombay.

The Gateway of India, seen from the upper floors of the Taj Hotel, was completed in 1928 to celebrate
the arrival of King George V and Queen Mary.

Land and People

"Though outwardly there was diversity and infinite variety among our people, every-where there was that tremendous impress of oneness, which had held all of us together for ages…some kind of a dream of unity has occupied the mind of India since the dawn of civilisation."

—Jawaharlal Nehru, first prime minister of independent India.

I ndia is vast. The world's seventh largest country, her landmass is over 3.28 million square kilometres (1.26 million square miles), an area as large and varied as Europe. Her coastlines run 5,650 kilometres (3,533 miles) and her frontiers with neighbours extend an astonishing 15,168 kilometres (9,425 miles). From the state of Jammu and Kashmir, her northern border with China, to her southern tip at Kanniyakumari ('the Abode of the Virgin Goddess'), the subcontinent stretches from 38 degrees north latitude, well above the Tropic of Cancer, to just 7 degrees above the equator.

Within this span lies every type of physical terrain. To the north rise the mighty Himalayas (*hima* meaning 'snow'; *laya* meaning 'abode'), the world's highest mountain range and the largest area covered by snow and ice outside of the poles. The many Himalayan valleys flow with sparkling rivers and are clothed with flowers and forests of pine, juniper, deodar and silver birch, while lush thickets of banana and rustling

Page 17: Mehrangarh Fort, founded in 1459, stands on a 150-metre (165-foot) hill overlooking and dominating the Rajasthani city of Jodhpur. In the foreground is the Jaswant Thada, a cluster of royal cenotaphs in white marble built in 1899 in memory of Maharaja Jaswant Singh I.
Above: A Sikh temple guardian, or *nihang*, at the Golden Temple, Amritsar.

Above: A young Sikh girl during the annual procession of the Granth Sahib (the Sikh sacred book kept in the Golden Temple) around Amritsar.
Opposite: A group of tribal women from a village on the edge of the Thar desert in Rajasthan walk to the local well in the late afternoon to draw water.

Above: A Rajasthani woman drawing water from a desert well close to Khuri village, near Jaisalmer.

Village life in Rajasthan. **Left:** A painted doorway to a farm in Khuri.
Above: A turbaned man at the weekly market in Agolai, near Jodhpur.
Opposite: A calf in Khuri village, near Jaisalmer.

bamboo cover the foothills, where temperate zones are swathed in rhododendron, sal, oak, maple and birch. The western foothills trail off into the well-irrigated and prosperous Punjab, India's wheat basket and where the 'green revolution' took off in the 1960s. Further south stretches the Great Thar desert, covering the states of Western Rajasthan and Kutch—and 8 per cent of the country's surface—in sand dunes and rocky outcrops. To the east unfolds the lush alluvial plain of the River Ganges, the most densely populated area on earth. The Ganges meets her sister the Brahmaputra to enter the Bay of Bengal in a marshy delta lying below sea level, where mangrove forests spawn a wide variety of exotic flora and fauna.

India's great triangular central plateau, known as the Deccan, descends to the sea through low hills known as the Western and Eastern Ghats, which give way to thin coastal strips bordering the Arabian Sea to the west and the Bay of Bengal to the east. The Deccan, with geological strata several hundred million years old, is considered the oldest part of the country; coal, diamonds and gold are mined here. Finally converging towards the subcontinent's tip, the Ghats form the Nilgiri Hills, where much tea is grown. Below are India's two southernmost states, Kerala and Tamil Nadu, distant in everything but location. Kerala, on the western seaboard, is the verdant spice garden that first lured traders to India and has a polyglot culture shaped by Arab, Roman, Chinese, Dutch, British and Marxist influences. A relatively modernised state, her Christian community, a fourth of her

Left: The Darjeeling Himalayan Railway, nicknamed 'the toy train', is a narrow-gauge line serving the famous hill station in West Bengal from the town of Siliguri.
Opposite: Leaves being picked on the terraces of a tea plantation near Coonoor in the southern state of Tamil Nadu.

population, is the oldest outside of Israel and her 99 per cent literacy rate is five per cent higher than America's. To the east, Tamil Nadu is a bastion of traditional Hindu civilisation, boasting magnificent medieval temple-cities—treasure houses of art, culture and arcane ritual—rising like exotic carved islands from glittering emerald seas of paddy.

India's climate is as varied at her topography. A spectacular example: in 1969 most of Rajasthan had been without rain for 13 years, while parts of Assam, about 1,609 kilometres (1,000 miles) to the east, had no less than 21 metres (69 feet). The north and central regions enjoy four seasons. Winter (December–March), with sunny days and cool nights, is the best time to travel; spring (April–June), when the pre-monsoon tension builds up oppressively and temperatures can reach a gasping 50°C (122°F); Summer (June–September), when the monsoons finally break and the parched country enjoys an obligatory bath, followed by a brief autumn (September–November) sprinkled with fresh green shoots fanned by warm breezes. At this time a second monsoon begins to blow across southern India from the northeast, bringing rains that make this the greenest part of the subcontinent. Nowadays, however, global climatic changes make the monsoon increasingly unpredictable. This irregularity, coupled with the effects of widespread deforestation in most of the hill areas, leads to swings of drought and flood that can devastate the lives of millions. India is no stranger to Mother Nature's fickleness, and the

Left: A small traditional boat known as a *shikara* floats on Lake Dal in Kashmir, close to the capital Srinagar.
Opposite: An Indian farmer near Mysore leads his cow down to the river to bathe on a misty morning.

resultant fragility of life has been deeply etched onto the Indian psyche during the nation's long history.

Throughout this enormous terrain is spread the world's second largest population, over one billion people and increasing by more than 14 million each year. They come in every conceivable hue of skin and cut of feature, and between them speak no less than 17 major languages (each as different as the major European languages), 18 minor ones (each with its own script, grammar and cultural associations) and over 20,000 distinct dialects. Such linguistic variety poses daunting problems: even Hindi, the national language, is understood by less than half the country.

This richly differentiated people—which includes almost 70 million tribals, some of whom still live at Stone-Age level—is distributed between 26 semi-autonomous states and seven union territories. While each has its distinct traditions, dress, customs and cuisine, all owe allegiance to the central government at Delhi.

Ramshackle as this super-pluralist democracy may be as it lurches periodically from crisis to crisis, it continues on, sometimes surprising in a typically Indian way. Kerala, for example, was the first place in the world to freely elect a communist government, throw it out, and then re-elect it—all by fair ballot. Though the strains at the edges threaten to erupt, somehow the centre does hold, and 'Unity in diversity' has long been India's proud motto.

Left, top: A Bengali priest, centre, instructs the garlanded couple at a wedding ceremony in Kolkata.
Left: Male guests wearing distinctive local costumes that include a sash and decorative dagger at another wedding, this time in Coorg (Kodagu) in Karnataka's Western Ghats.
Opposite: A woman at the Mysore temple of Venugopalaswamy dons a sari.
Far opposite: Marigolds, used extensively for garlands throughout India, for sale at a flower market in Jaipur.

A misty morning near Manikarnika Ghat, Varanasi. Built on the banks of the sacred River Ganges (Ganga), Varanasi, also known as Banaras, Kashi, and 'the City of Light', is the world's oldest continuously inhabited city, ancient even at the time of the Buddha.

Close to Allahabad, the confluence of the Ganges, Yamuna and Saraswati rivers is popularly known as Triveni Sangam. Its sandbanks are a constant attraction for bathing pilgrims.

Sunrise attracts scores of ritual bathers beneath the Howrah Bridge, further down the Ganges in Kolkata.
Following page: Lake Pichola in the city of Udaipur. The white artificial island is the famous Lake Palace Hotel, built as a summer palace in the seventeenth century by the ruler Jagat Singh. Facing it to the right is the City Palace.

History

"All the convergent influences of the world run through this society: Hindu, Muslim, Christian, secular; Stalinist, liberal, Maoist, democratic socialist, Gandhian. There is not a thought that is being thought in the West or East that is not active in some Indian mind."

—E.P. Thompson, twentieth-century English historian.

As a glance at the map makes clear, India's history is her geography. Her funnel-shaped landmass is closed by an impenetrable 2,897 kilometre (1,800 mile) mountain chain to the northeast, surrounded by water to the south, west and east, and open only on its northwest flank. It is this penetrable northwest frontier that has provided the route for overland foreign invaders from earliest times, each influx creating its own place in the highly variegated mosaic that is India.

Although much early Indian history is far from certain, the first invaders we know of were the Aryans, pastoral nomads from the central Asian steppes, who entered the subcontinent in a series of waves starting in about 2000 BC. They brought with them many features of what was later to become the religion we call Hinduism—the sacred language of Sanskrit, esoteric rituals, reverence for the cow, the caste system and the Vedas, scriptures the orthodox Hindu continues to hold in the highest esteem. The Aryans (meaing 'noble') settled across North India, especially along the fertile

Gangetic plain. The light-skinned Aryans were of very different ethnic stock to the indigenous people they met. Among these were the members of the highly sophisticated Indus Valley civilisation. In existence for perhaps 1,500 years, this civilisation had traded with ancient Mesopotamia and built astonishingly well-organized cities such as Harappa and Mohenjodaro, as well as more than one hundred other settlements. Another important group was the Dravidians—smaller, darker people who had also formed an ancient culture and are now found predominantly in southern India.

The basis of much of modern India can be explained as a mixture of these initial civilisations, but decisive as the Aryan invasion was, it was only the first of many that streamed through the Khyber Pass. Next came the Persians, under such famous warrior-leaders as Cyrus and Darius (521–485 BC), who the brought formative ideas such as sun worship and the divinity of the monarch. Alexander the Great reached the Indus in 328 BC and, according to legend, met a speaking tree that prophesied not only that he would never conquer India, but also that he would never see his homeland again. The tree was right: he died travelling back to Greece to collect more troops for an invasion. Though he never conquered the country, he left behind him artists and sculptors who introduced Greek artistic ideals that flowered in the Buddhist art of the Gandhara school, located in the Hellenic province of Bactria, in what is now northern Afghanistan and Pakistan.

Previous page: The cave paintings at Ajanta, dating to the fifth and sixth centuries AD, are considered masterpieces of Buddhist religious art.
Right: Kailash temple, Ellora, is arguably the greatest rock-cut temple in the world. It was commissioned around AD 760 by the Rashtrakuta king Krishna I, and carved beginning at the top.

The main resistance to Greek incursions was offered by the powerful Magadha kingdom, ruled most notably by Chandragupta, who ascended the throne in 320 BC. Around this time in the country's northeast, the egalitarian teachings of the Buddha (died c. 450 BC) were exerting a tremendous influence on the development of Indian society. Buddhism was consolidated by the conversion and patronage of Chandragupta's grandson, Ashoka (269–232 BC)—ruler of the Mauryan Empire—and its civilising influence persisted until the arrival of the Muslims over one thousand years later.

Other invaders followed—Scythians and Parthians from Persia, Kushanas and White Huns from Central Asia—but this turmoil did not prevent the flourishing of the remarkable Gupta dynasty in eastern India, ruled by Chandragupta and his son Samudragupta (third to fourth centuries AD), who generously patronized religion, art and learning to create a golden age of Indian civilisation.

The most profound impact on India's history came from Islam's arival. First were peaceful Arab traders who landed on the west coast as early as the seventh century AD, followed by a series of raids by assorted freebooters lured by tales of the fabulous riches of the Indian courts. The most ruthless was an Afghan named Mahmud of Ghazni, who invaded India no fewer than 17 times between 1000 and 1027. Mahmud devastated much of North India, destroying temples and looting cities wherever he went, but he did patronize Islamic culture—the great poet Firdausi and the famous historian al-Biruni were part of his court. Then in 1192 came the consolidation

Built by the Mughal emperor Akbar, Fatehpur Sikri was abandoned by 1584, within years of its completion. Its style is Indo-Islamic—a fusion of native Indian and imported Islamic. **Left:** The Diwan-i Khass, or 'private audience hall'. **Opposite:** The Astrologer's Seat.

of Islamic influence. An Afghan named Muhammad of Ghor took the Punjab and then Delhi, and Islam had come to stay. The Hindu kingdoms were disunited, and according to caste rules only the warrior groups were able to fight. Moreover, the Muslims had archers and, most importantly, the horse, while traditional Indian armies relied on the powerful but cumbersome elephant and foot soldiers armed with lances and swords. The Turk, Afghan or Mongol was often bigger than his opponent; this advantage of size, in the service of crusaders' zeal and plunderers' greed, made them unstoppable.

A series of Islamic sultanates, with Delhi as their capital, ruled the north until the decisive establishment of the Mughal dynasty in 1526. Through a succession of 6 great rulers, the Mughals gave much of North India its recognizable face. Humayun (1530–1556) introduced Persian influences—music, poetry, delicate floral motifs in art, soaring domes and elegant arches in architecture and Persian replaced Sanskrit as the language of the imperial court. His son Akbar (1556–1605), the greatest of the Mughal emperors, was unstinting in his patronage of artists, scholars and clerics, tolerantly supporting all religions and bequeathing to his son Jahangir (1605–1627) a love of nature, art and literature. Jahangir laid out many beautiful gardens throughout his kingdom, and it was his son, Shah Jahan (1627–1658) who, as well as raising elegant capitals at Lahore, Agra and Delhi, built the Taj Mahal, justly celebrated to this day as India's supreme symbol and the world's most beautiful building.

Right: A fusion of Persian, Central Asian and Islamic architecture, the Taj Mahal houses the tombs of Shah Jahan and his wife Mumtaz Mahal.
Opposite: The Taj Mahal's symmetry is emphasised by the long reflecting pool in front.

While all these foreign influences were shaping the north, the Deccan and the south were left relatively untouched and free to develop through the economic and military rivalry of a number of successive and overlapping Dravidian dynasties. The Deccani dynasties of the Chalukyas (450–700) and Hoysalas (1100–1300) are remembered today chiefly for developing the form of the Hindu temple, while in Tamil Nadu, the mighty Pallavas (600–850) established a capital at Kanchipuram and ports at modern Madras (Chennai) and Mahabalipuram that served an extensive maritime empire. This took Hindu culture as far as Indonesia; its influence can still be seen on the island of Bali, at sites such as Prambanan in central Java and in the widespread popularity of the Ramayana epic throughout the archipelago. The Pallavas gave way to the Cholas (900–1100); their capital, Tanjore, was the nerve centre of another mighty empire that stretched from the Gangetic plain to Sri Lanka, and they extended southeast Asian trading contacts as far as China. Then came the Pandyas (1150–1350), who ruled from the sacred temple-city Madurai, still one of the gems of South Indian architecture. The last great dynasty of the south, famed for its prolonged and heroic resistance to Muslim incursions, was that of Vijayanagar (1336–1565), centred at the extended capital of Hampi, truly one of the architectural wonders of the subcontinent.

A new and decisive chapter began with the arrival of the Europeans, who sought lucrative spices. First were the Portuguese. The explorer Vasco da Gama arrived at Calicut (from which we get our word calico) in 1497; by the time he left five years later he had established a Portuguese trading presence on the western coast and a fleet to protect it. The Portuguese captured Goa in 1510 (it remained their colony until 1961), but it was the arrival of the

The elaborate carved decoration, screens and inlay work of Itmad-ud-Daulah's tomb are all typical of Islamic style.
Above: Details of pietra dura work. **Opposite:** A pierced marble screen.

British that was to prove the most significant. News that the Dutch had made a 2,500 per cent profit on a cargo of spices from Indonesia prompted the founding of the British East India Company (EIC) in 1601. Beaten out of the Indonesian spice islands by the superior navy of the Dutch, the fledgling company focused on India; little did those involved at the time realize that the seed of empire had silently been sown. It was EIC trade in pepper, cloves and cardamom from Kerala, silk from Bengal, cotton from Maharashtra, and saltpetre and indigo dye from Gujerat that led to the establishment of company warehouses, known as 'factories,' in Chennai (1640) and Mumbai (1668), and the creation of the port of Kolkata (1690). Little by little, these settlements grew, protected by forts and locally recruited militia known as *sepoys*. A series of tactical alliances with local rulers added to the inexorable advance of British influence.

Encouraged by India's 2,414-kilometre (1,500-mile) western seaboard, with its strong currents and abundance of natural harbours, other European powers established trading interests as well. By the mid-eighteenth century, with the decadence and collapse of the centralized Mughal empire, a power vacuum had appeared in which the main contenders for supremacy were clearly France and Britain, both already at war in Europe. Largely due to the military acumen and efforts of Robert Clive, himself a former clerk of the EIC, the French were defeated in a series of battles—the most important being Plessey in 1757—that put

Humayun's Tomb in Delhi, India. Humayun, the eldest son of the Mughal empire's first emperor, Babur, succeeded his father. Humayun's Tomb was the first garden tomb made in India.

Bengal, a key trading area, under British control and ended French aspirations in India.

It was in Bengal that the EIC first gained control of local revenue collection. This marked a crucial advance, as it allowed them to pay for commodities locally without relying on gold and silver bullion from home. The early nineteenth century saw further penetration of British influence—particularly in the teaching of the English language, the promotion of Christianity and the setting up of an English-language legal system. But EIC corruption, the levelling of taxes that were invariable (rather than proportionate to the harvest yield) and the import of cheap mass-produced goods from industrial Britain damaged local industry and alienated Indian opinion. This situation culminated in 1857 in what might be known as the Sepoy Revolt, the Indian Mutiny or the First War of Independence, depending on one's viewpoint. This short but bloody war shocked Victorian Britain to the core, and a new chapter in British-Indian relations began. The Crown officially took over rule of India from the EIC, which went ignominiously bankrupt a few years later; the office of viceroy was created; the size of the army was doubled and the Indian Civil Service formed (the highest ranks in both were denied to Indians); new roads, railways and bridges were built; and the universities of Mumbai (Bombay), Calcuatta and Madras were founded to promulgate English education and values.

An independence movement stirred as early as 1885 with the founding of the Indian National Congress by a group of loosely affiliated but disaffected intellectuals, but it was the 1905 plan to divide Bengal into two parts, one Hindu and the other Muslim, that first really united Indian opposition to British rule. Though the resultant campaign of strikes and demonstrations was quashed, the seed had been sown. In 1911 the imperial capital was moved from Kolkata to Delhi, an event celebrated by the magnificent visit of George V and Queen Mary. Four years later, a Gujerati lawyer educated in England returned to India from South Africa, where he had been active in the fight against racial intolerance. This was Mahatma ('Great Soul') Gandhi, who became known as 'Father of the Nation' for his nonviolent struggle for independence based on economic self-sufficiency and traditional village autonomy. Part saint, part wily politician, Gandhi was not to see his dream of a peaceful transfer of power realized, but he acted as a figurehead to unite his countrymen in a campaign of peaceful civil disobedience that was as revolutionary as it was successful.

After the Second World War the agitation for independence reached fever pitch as violence erupted between Hindu and Muslim communities, especially those in northern India, due to the demands for a separate state for Muslims made by the Muslim League, led by Mohammed Ali Jinnah. Faced with the prospect of an imminent civil war, it was decided that the subcontinent would be partitioned to create two new countries: Pakistan—originally divided into West and East Pakistan—was for Muslims, and India was for a predominantly Hindu population. The result was a disaster. Perhaps 1.5 million people died in intercommunal bloodshed while a further 13 million refugees, many from the Punjab

Opposite: Mumbai, late in developing a distinct architecture, benefited from the work of many talented British architects who worked in the Indo-Saracenic style.
Right: The statue of Queen Victoria, also Empress of India, in front of the Victoria Memorial in Kolkata. Work on the memorial, designed by Sir William Emerson, began in 1904, but its completion was delayed until 1921.

and the Gangetic plain, desperately sought to escape the mayhem and rebuild their lives in unfamiliar and inhospitable surroundings. It was during this chaos that the last viceroy, Lord Mountbatten, stepped down on 15 August, 1947, and India achieved her independence. This bittersweet chapter in a great nation's history ended with a tragedy: early in 1948 Mahatma Gandhi was assassinated by a Hindu fanatic for being too conciliatory to the Muslims.

In the years since independence, the Indian political scene has been dominated by the Congress Party, which followed the socialist model of a controlled economy for almost 50 years. Congress was led by a family dynasty: the first prime minister, Jawaharlal Nehru, was succeeded by his daughter Indira Gandhi in 1964. Assassinated by Sikhs in 1984, she was succeeded by her son Rajiv, until in 1991 he, too, was assassinated, but by Tamils. Both leaders paid the price for their handling of extremist groups wanting independence from the centre. Since the defeat of the Congress Party in 1996, the country has had a succession of short-term and coalition governments, which have increasingly opened India to multinationals and the free market. Significantly, recent years have seen the rise of Hindu nationalism. Today Indians maintain their passionate interest in politics but also a healthy scepticism towards those who strut and struggle for their brief moment of power, for hasn't a country with such a venerable and volatile history seen it all before?

Opposite: The Lotus Mahal at Vijayanagara in northern Karnataka.
Right: A granite column at the Vitthala temple in the Vijyanagara complex, with the Garuda shrine in the form of a chariot behind.

"As space pervades a jar, both inside and out,
so within and beyond this ever-changing
universe there exists one Cosmic Intelligence."

—Shiva Samhita, sixth-century religious text.

Religion and Ritual

The Indians are above all a religious people, and there is not a religion in the world that has not found sanctuary here at some time or other, and stayed on to prosper. Jews came in the sixth century BC, following the destruction of their temple in Jerusalem; St Thomas the Apostle brought Christianity in the first century AD; while 600 years later Zoroastrians (known as Parsees) fled here when Arabs ravished their native Persia. And India herself is the birthplace of four major religions: Hinduism, Buddhism, Jainism and Sikhism.

Today, Muslims constitute 12 per cent of India's population (a higher per cent than in Pakistan!). She is also home to 22 million Christians, 18 million Sikhs, 12 million Buddhists and Jains, and perhaps half a million Parsees. But her population is overwhelmingly Hindu, at 82 per cent.

The word *Hinduism* is a western import coined to cover the huge variety of religious belief and practice found in the subcontinent, called by the Indians themselves *Sanatana Dharma*: 'the Eternal Law'. Hinduism has no historical founder, no one authority, no single organizing body; it is not so much a religion as a way of life that guides its followers from conception to the funeral pyre. And even beyond, for the Hindu believes that we reincarnate life after life, until we have fulfilled our task of achieving enlightenment.

Most outsiders' first reaction to Hinduism is one of confusion. Such rampant polytheism seems over the top: dozens of gods and goddesses, some with animal heads and human bodies, sprout heads and arms with a positively irreligious abandon. To the Hindu, however, all these divinities are but partial symbolic expressions of one universal, cosmic intelligence known as Brahman, which upholds all life. This supreme intelligence is abstract, formless, and not directly accessible to worship, though the yogi and saint can experience it through meditation and devotion. Inexpressible, it expresses itself through all the phenomena of the universe. It is said there are as many ways to approach Brahman as there are people wanting to approach it; thus the different divinities, each embodying aspects of this one intelligence, cater to the unending variety of seekers and draw them to it. Thus we are attracted to the deity that represents characteristics we may be in need of, or is suited to where we are in

Previous page: Close to Palitana in Gujarat, Shatrunjaya, or 'the Place of Victory', is a mountain complex of temples sacred to the Jain religion, which was founded before 1000 BC and stresses nonviolence and vegetarianism.
Left: A Mysore woman, accompanied by her daughter, makes an offering in front of a sacred tree at Venugopalaswamy temple, Mysore.
Opposite: The temple of Arunachaleshvara and the surrounding town of Tiruvannamalai seen from the hill dwelling of a *sadhu* (holy man). The temple, one of the largest in India, is dedicated to lord Shiva.

our life's journey. There is no sense of exclusivity; indeed, the traditionally pious Hindu may be devoted to three different levels of deity—local god (gramadevata), family god (kula-devata), and personal, chosen god (ishta-devata)—with no conflict between them.

The Hindu pantheon is thus as vast and as multifarious as the country itself. Its many deities have both fierce and gentle forms, consorts and children, attendants and vehicles. There are three principle members, however, each personifying a different phase of the cosmic evolutionary process: Brahma, the creator; Vishnu, the preserver; and Shiva, the transformer.

Brahma, although figuring largely in the Puranas, the main texts describing the cosmic escapades of the gods, is hardly worshipped at all today; only two temples to him are active. His consort, Saraswati, the goddess of learning, music and artistic activity, is largely a domestic deity, worshipped in the homes of artists, intellectuals and students.

Vishnu, by contrast, is widely popular. His followers, known as Vaishnavas, are often distinguished by V-shaped marks on their foreheads which represent the god's feet. Associated with the life of the householder, Vishnu has two consorts: Shri Devi, goddess of good fortune, and Bhu Devi, mother earth. He also has ten major incarnations that are born on earth when needed to right the imbalance between good and evil. Two of these are especially popular across north and central India. The seventh, Rama, is the ideal ruler and hero of the Ramayana, one of the two great epics (the other is the Mahabharata), that have gripped the Indian imagination for millennia. The eighth is Krishna, god of love. One of India's favourite scriptures, the Bhagavad Gita, describes Krishna as the wise and compassionate teacher of humanity, while much of the north's folk

Opposite: A poster hanging in a shop is one of countless depictions of Ganesh, the elephant-headed son of Shiva. The popularity of this deity is undoubtedly connected to the belief that he is the god of education, knowledge, wisdom and wealth.

Above: The afternoon procession of the images of Balaji (Vishnu) and his consort around the temple of Tirumala, in Andhra Pradesh.

Right: The ornate western gopuram (gate) of Sri Meenakshi temple in Madurai.

music, poetry and particularly miniature painting celebrates his mischievous youth, his amorous dalliances with the cowgirls and his great love for Radha, his chief consort. As the ideal couple, together they represent a paradigm of romantic sexual love between humans and, at another level, the yearning of the soul for God.

Shiva, the third member of the trinity, combines many contrasts. He is the archetypal yogi, deity of recluses and celibates, meditating in solitude in the Himalayan snows or wandering dishevelled amidst smouldering funeral pyres, counselling his followers to meditate on the transience of all life. Yet he is also Nataraja, lord of the cosmic dance, creating and transforming universes in a wild dance of bliss, his long hair flying out behind him in an uninhibited Dionysian revel. And sometimes he is the great lover, who gets into trouble for seducing the wives of pious sages and flies into a rage when thwarted. Shiva's main consort is Parvati, the idealized feminine deity, the graceful and gentle companion of her lord's pleasures. Followers of Shiva are known as Shaivas, and wear three white horizontal lines on their foreheads. Shiva temples tend to be more numerous in the south.

Another important deity is Shakti, the feminine force personified in countless forms, many quite localized. Examples of these are the mother goddess; the fierce goddesses Kali (often associated with Shiva) and her invincible sister, Durga; and the Seven Mothers, who are worshipped in villages all over the country. There are also a host of local goddesses, such as Shitala, goddess of fevers; Annapurna,

An annual bathing ceremony at the twelfth-century temple of Venugopalaswamy, near the Cauvery River in Mysore, dedicated to lord Vishnu.

goddess of nourishment; and Ganga Ma, goddess of the life-giving River Ganges.

One more kind of god should be mentioned: those deities that link the divine, human and animal kingdoms. Ganesh, the elephant-headed son of Parvati, is universally loved as the god of good beginnings, while Hanuman, the monkey god and lord Rama's attendant and general in the Ramayana, is the epitome of devotion, courage and loyalty.

Along with these classical figures, village Hinduism incorporates archaic strata of ancient worship centred on natural phenomena such as snakes, mountains, trees and rivers. This sits quite comfortably with the later, more sophisticated pantheon celebrated in temple and canonical literature, combining with them to create a vibrantly sacred universe operating on many interconnected levels.

Despite the great variety of gods, rituals of worship are fairly standard. When the Hindus worship an image, they are entertaining a royal guest and fulfilling its physical needs. The scale of such worship can be staggering, continuing for hours and involving hundreds of priests and officiates. This is especially true in the south, where temple ritual has been preserved intact over the millennia. At the major annual festival at the great Vishnu temple of Tirupati in Andhra Pradesh, for example, 32 types of flowers are offered, weighing almost 2,500 kilograms (5,500 lbs).

Ordinary temple worship (*puja*) takes place four times a day at sunrise, noon, sunset and midnight, though often only the morning and evening sessions are observed. The worship is performed by the

Opposite: The Church of Our Lady of the Immaculate Conception in Panjim, Goa.
Right: Cleaning a statue.

Left: Sikh temple guardians, or nihang, at the Golden Temple in Amritsar on the occasion of the annual parade during which the Granth Sahib, the Sikh sacred book, is carried through the city.

Above: The Golden Temple, set in the Lake of Ambrosia, is the centre of the Sikh world. It was founded in 1589 on an island in this small lake known since the time of the Buddha as a special site and a place of healing.

Architecture

"A religious patron will always have peace, wealth, grain and sons. Everything vanishes in time; only a religious monument lasts for ever."

—Shilpa Prakasha, ancient architectural text.

At the same tim[...]
India, the early mo[...]
were excavating roc[...]
their lives of medita[...]
the Buddhist caves[...]
manmade caves, son[...]
itable cathedrals Pa[...]
dating from the Gu[...]
Buddhist art. Glowi[...]
scenes from the J[...]
Nearby, the comple[...]
and Jain—includin[...]
Temple (AD 750). Its[...]
5 million pounds)[...]
constitute an encyc[...]

The Hindu ten[...]
the gods, where wo[...]
The first freestandin[...]
glean an idea of the[...]
such as Nepal an[...]
recently remained[...]
Shastras, sacred ar[...]
patrons and builde[...]

Page 65: The Palace [...]
Sawai Pratap Singh. L[...]
storey façade feature[...]
Opposite and right: [...]
from the second and[...]
site was discovered [...]

Among the astonishing richness of architectural remains in India, the earliest we have are examples in various states of repair of the Buddhist relic mound known as the *stupa*. These hemispherical domes were first erected to enshrine the ashes of the Buddha himself, and later those of great Buddhist teachers. The most spectacular is the restored Great Stupa of Sanchi, near Bhopal in Madhya Pradesh, which dates from the third century BC when the emperor Ashoka laid its foundation stone. Surrounded by railings punctuated at the cardinal points by sandstone gates with beautiful carvings telling the story of Buddhism, Sanchi shows us the prototype of a structure that was exported wherever Buddhism went. Sri Lanka, the Himalayas, Southeast Asia and the Far East all developed their own versions of what has come to be Buddhism's major contribution to world architecture.

Right: Coloured glass windows face the sunrise in the Kush Mahal suite at the famous Lake Palace Hotel.
Above: The Lake Palace Hotel launch ferries guests to and from the landing stage. The hotel was originally built as a summer palace, the Jag Niwas, on an artificial island in the middle of the lake.

For some the memory will be of that wedding party, where the women—hung with gold and gliding along like stately galleons with the stiff rustle of fine new silk—invited you to join the celebration; for others it may be that temple festival when a cow decorated with vermilion and marigolds led a procession of anarchic musicians and dancing devotees covered only by their long, matted hair and ochre loincloths.

Whatever your memories, they will confirm the fact that India is incorrigibly various. There is not one India but myriads, happily co-existing, with people doing their own thing within a loose framework of broad rules. Here there is no boring standardisation, no fixed stereotype. Whatever statement is made about the place, the opposite is also true: India delights in providing a host of exceptions to every rule. So those who wish to understand the country must bring an open mind and an ability to be flexible, for India will be relentless in her demands for both. But the rewards are well worth it. India is like nowhere else; a living dream in which everything is possible. Once you have visited her, your life will never be the same, and she will have cast her spell on you forever.

Luxury tented accommodation at Vanyavilas on the edge of the Ranthambore Tiger Reserve. A far cry from the concept of simply camping, these tents are fitted to five-star standards.

SELECTED FURTHER READING

Freedom at Midnight. Larry Collins & Dominique Lapierre. London: HarperCollins, 1997.

The Hindu Temple. George Michel. Chicago: University of Chicago Press, 1988.

India: A History. John Keay. London: HarperCollins Publishers, 2001.

India Modern. Michael Freeman. Singapore: Periplus Editions, 2005.

India: A Wounded Civilization. V. S. Naipaul. London: Picador, 2002.

Indian Art. Vidya Dehejia. London: Phaidon, 1998.

Introduction to Indian Architecture. Bindia Thapar, Surat Kumar Manto, and Suparna Bhalla. Singapore: Periplus Editions, 2005.

Lonely Planet India. Sarina Singh, et al. London: Lonely Planet Publications, 2007.

A Passage to India. E. M. Forster. London: Penguin Books, 1998.

Plain Tales from the Raj. Charles Allen (ed). London: Abacus, 1988.

The Ramayana. R. K. Narayan. London: Penguin, 2006.

The Rough Guide to India. Nick Edwards, et al. London: Rough Guides, 2005.

Slowly Down the Ganges. Eric Newby. London: Picador, 1983.